BOTANICAL SANCTUARIES

North Dakota Ecoregions

- Northwestern Great Plains
- Northwestern Glaciated Plains
- Northern Glaciated Plains
- Lake Agassiz Plain

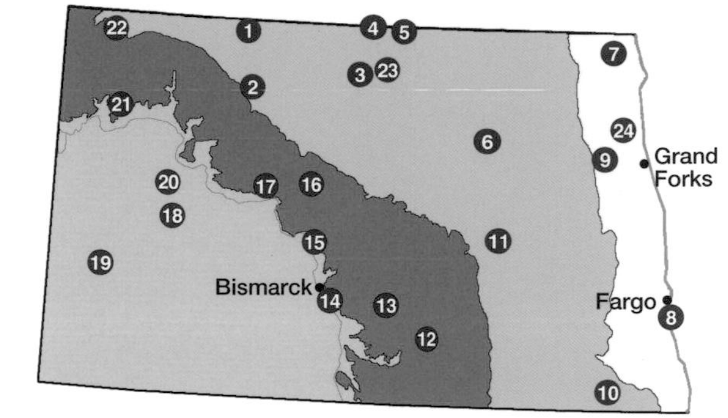

Grand Forks
Bismarck
Fargo

1. Des Lacs National Wildlife Refuge (NWR)
2. Lostwood NWR
3. J. Clark Salyer NWR
4. Lake Metigoshe State Park
5. International Peace Garden
6. Black Tiger Bay State Recreation Area
7. Gunlogson Arboretum Nature Preserve
8. Northern Plains Botanic Garden Society
9. Turtle River State Park
10. Tewaukon NWR
11. Arrowwood NWR
12. Beaver Lake State Park
13. Long Lake NWR
14. Fort Abraham Lincoln State Park
15. Cross Ranch State Park
16. Audubon NWR
17. Fort Stevenson State Park Arboretum
18. Lake Ilo National Wildlife Preserve
19. Theodore Roosevelt National Park
20. Little Missouri State Park
21. Lewis & Clark State Park
22. Crosby Wetland Management District
23. Denbigh Experimental Forest
24. Myra Arboretum

Measurements denote the height of plants unless otherwise indicated. Illustrations are not to scale.

N.B. – Many edible wild plants have poisonous mimics. Never eat a wild plant or fruit unless you are absolutely sure it is safe to do so. The publisher makes no representation or warranties with respect to the accuracy, completeness, correctness or usefulness of this information and specifically disclaims any implied warranties of fitness for a particular purpose. The advice, strategies and/or techniques contained herein may not be suitable for all individuals. The publisher shall not be responsible for any physical harm (up to and including death), loss of profit or other commercial damage. The publisher assumes no liability brought or instituted by individuals or organizations arising out of or relating in any way to the application and/or use of the information, advice and strategies contained herein.

Waterford Press produces reference guides that introduce novices to nature, science, travel and languages. Product information is featured on the website: **www.waterfordpress.com**

Scan for more info

Made in the USA

Text and illustrations © 2010, 2017 by Waterford Press Inc. All rights reserved. Cover images © Shutterstock. Ecoregion map © The National Atlas of the United States.

To order, call 800-434-2555. For permissions, or to share comments, e-mail editor@waterfordpress.com. For information on custom-published products, call 800-434-2555 or e-mail info@waterfordpress.com.

ISBN 978-1-58355-515-6 $7.95 U.S.

9 781583 555156 50795

UPC 8 84682 01073 7

10 9 8 7 6 5 4 3 2 1 700142

NORTH DAKOTA TREES & WILDFLOWERS – A Folding Pocket Guide to Familiar Plants Kavanagh/Leung

A POCKET NATURALIST® GUIDE

NORTH DAKOTA TREES & WILDFLOWERS

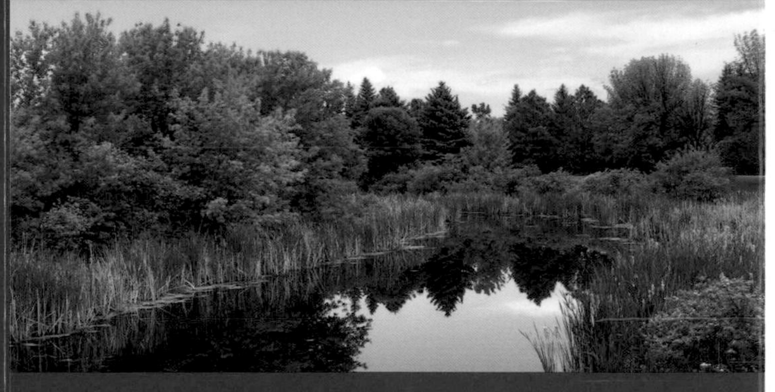

A Folding Pocket Guide to Familiar Plants

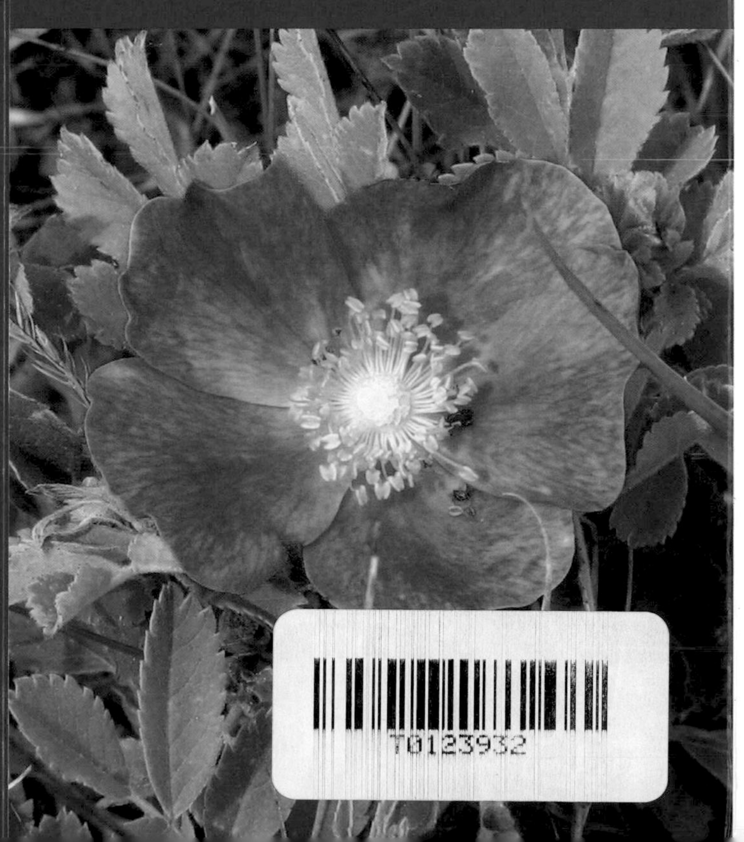

T0123932

TREES & SHRUBS

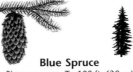

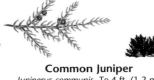

Limber Pine
Pinus flexilis To 50 ft. (15 m)
Needles grow in bundles of 5. Elongate cone has scales thickest at their tips.

Tamarack
Larix spp. To 80 ft. (24 m)
Needles grow in tufts. Stalkless cones grow upright. One of the only conifers to shed its needles in winter.

Eastern Cottonwood
Populus deltoides To 100 ft. (30 m)
Leaves are up to 7 in. (18 cm) long. Flowers are succeeded by capsules containing seeds with cottony 'tails'.

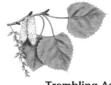

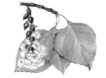

Paper Birch
Betula papyrifera To 70 ft. (21 m)
Whitish bark peels off trunk in thin sheets. Bark was used by Native Americans to make bowls and canoes.

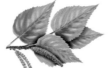

Siberian Elm
Ulmus pumila To 60 ft. (18 m)
Introduced tree has small leaves with short stems. Flowers bloom in drooping clusters of 2-5 and are succeeded by single-winged seeds.

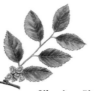

Bur Oak
Quercus macrocarpa To 80 ft. (24 m)
Leaves have 5-9 lobes and are widest above the middle. The acorn cup is fringed.

Blue Spruce
Picea pungens To 100 ft. (30 m)
Blue-green needles are up to 1.5 in. (4 cm) long and very prickly. Cones have scales with ragged edges.

Trembling Aspen
Populus tremuloides To 70 ft. (21 m)
Long-stemmed leaves rustle in the slightest breeze. The most widely distributed tree in North America.

Peachleaf Willow
Salix amygdaloides To 60 ft. (18 m)
Tree has narrow, finely saw-toothed leaves that are hairy below.

American Elm
Ulmus americana To 100 ft. (30 m)
Note vase-shaped profile. Leaves are toothed. Fruits have a papery collar and are notched at the tip.
North Dakota's state tree.

Crabapple
Malus spp. To 30 ft. (9 m)
White to pinkish flowers bloom in late spring and are succeeded by small apples.

Boxelder
Acer negundo To 60 ft. (18 m)
Leaves have 3-7 leaflets. Seeds are encased in paired papery keys.

TREES & SHRUBS

American Basswood
Tilia americana To 100 ft. (30 m)
Leaves are heart-shaped. Flowers and nutlets hang from narrow leafy bracts. Often multi-trunked. Also called linden.

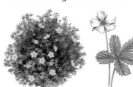

Common Chokecherry
Prunus virginiana To 20 ft. (6 m)
Cylindrical clusters of spring flowers are succeeded by dark, red-purple berries which are
North Dakota's state fruit.

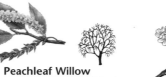

Hawthorn
Crataegus spp. To 40 ft. (12 m)
Tree has rounded crown of spiny branches. Apple-like fruits appear in summer.

Hackberry
Celtis occidentalis To 90 ft. (27 m)
Leaves are slightly toothed and curved at the tip. Red to purple fruits grow singly at the end of long stems.

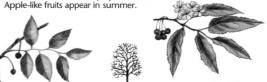

Ohio Buckeye
Aesculus glabra To 70 ft. (21 m)
Leaves have finger-like leaflets. Yellowish flowers bloom in erect clusters in spring. Fruit contains seeds that have a light 'eye' spot.

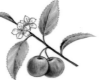

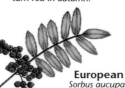

Black Walnut
Juglans nigra To 90 ft. (27 m)
Leaves have 9-23 leaflets. Greenish fruits have a black nut inside.

Beaked Hazelnut
Corylus cornuta To 10 ft. (3 m)
Sheathed, nut-like fruit matures into edible filberts by autumn.

Russian Olive
Elaeagnus angustifolia To 20 ft. (6 m)
Shrub or small tree has silvery leaves and spiny thorns. A fast-growing plant that was widely planted in shelterbelts.

Green Ash
Fraxinus pennsylvanica To 60 ft. (18 m)
Leaves have 7-9 leaflets. Flowers are succeeded by single-winged fruits.

Pin Cherry
Prunus pensylvanica To 30 ft. (9 m)
Lance-shaped leaves have curled margins. Small clusters of whitish flowers are succeeded by bright red berries.

Caragana
Caragana arborescens To 15 ft. (4.5 m)
Introduced shrub has pea-like seed pods. Likely the most widely planted shrub in the state.

American Plum
Prunus americana To 30 ft. (9 m)
Oval leaves have toothed edges. Bright red fruits have yellow flesh.

TREES & SHRUBS

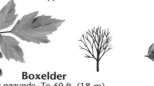

Big Sagebrush
Artemisia tridentata To 20 ft. (6 m)
Gray-green shrub has 3-toothed, wedge-shaped leaves. Bark is gray and shredding. Plant has odor of sage.

Common Juniper
Juniperus communis To 4 ft. (1.2 m)
Needle-like leaves grow in whorls of 3 around twigs. Berry-like, blue-black cones have 1-3 seeds.

Shrubby Cinquefoil
Potentilla fruticosa To 3 ft. (90 cm)
Small shrubby plant has bright yellow, waxy flowers.

Silverberry
Elaeagnus commutata
To 12 ft. (3.6 m)
Stiff, curled leaves have a shiny, silvery surface.

Western Serviceberry
Amelanchier alnifolia
To 30 ft. (9 m)
White, star-shaped flowers bloom in June and are succeeded by juicy, purple-black berries.

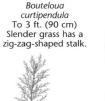

Silver Buffaloberry
Shepherdia argentea
To 16 ft. (4.8 m)
Leaves are fuzzy beneath with silvery hairs.

American Cranberry
Viburnum trilobum
To 15 ft. (4.5 m)
Flowers and fruits occur in large clusters. Native to moist areas around the state.

Purple Lilac
Syringa vulgaris
To 2.5 in. (6 cm)

Poison Ivy
Toxicodendron radicans
To 8 ft. (2.4 m)
Flowers bloom in loose clusters. Three-part leaves turn red in autumn.

Smooth Sumac
Rhus glabra
To 20 ft. (6 m)
Clusters of white flowers are succeeded by 'hairy' red fruits. Bark is gray and smooth.

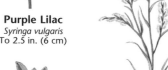

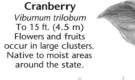

Kinnikinnick
Arctostaphylos uva-ursi
To 12 in. (30 cm)
Pinkish, bell-shaped flowers are succeeded by red-orange, mealy berries. Also known as bearberry.

European Mountain-ash
Sorbus aucuparia To 40 ft. (12 m)
Introduced ornamental is an important winter food source for birds. Leaves have 9-15 leaflets.

GRASSES

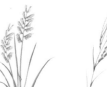

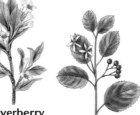

Big Blue Stem
Andropogon gerardii
To 7 ft. (2.1 m)
3-part seed head looks like a turkey's foot.

Blue Grama
Bouteloua gracilis
To 20 in. (50 cm)
Seed head looks like short-stalked 'eyebrows'.

Side-oats Grama
Bouteloua curtipendula
To 3 ft. (90 cm)
Slender grass has a zig-zag-shaped stalk.

Buffalo Grass
Buchloe dactyloides
To 12 in. (30 cm)

Canada Wild Rye
Elymus canadensis
To 4 ft. (1.2 m)

June Grass
Koeleria macrantha
To 2 ft. (60 cm)

Switch Grass
Panicum virgatum
To 8 ft. (2.4 m)

Western Wheatgrass
Pascopyrum smithii
To 3 ft. (90 cm)
North Dakota's state grass.

Little Bluestem
Schizachyrium scoparium
To 4 ft. (1.2 m)

Indian Grass
Sorghastrum nutans
To 8 ft. (2.4 m)

Prairie Cordgrass
Spartina pectinata
To 7 ft. (2.1 m)

Needle-and-thread
Stipa comata
To 10 ft. (3 m)
Needle-like seed looks liked a threaded sewing needle.

Needlegrass
Stipa spartea
To 7 ft. (2.1 m)
Note long bristles.

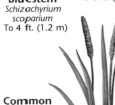

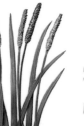

Common Cattail
Typha latifolia
To 10 ft. (3 m)

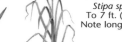

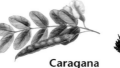

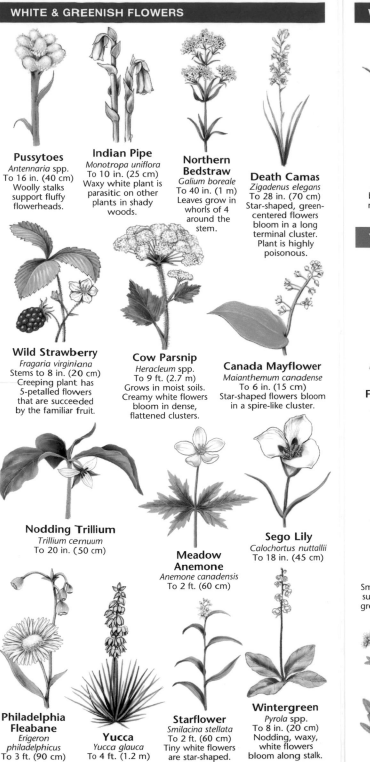

Pussytoes
Antennaria spp.
To 16 in. (40 cm)
Woolly stalks support fluffy flowerheads.

Indian Pipe
Monotropa uniflora
To 10 in. (25 cm)
Waxy white plant is parasitic on other plants in shady woods.

Northern Bedstraw
Galium boreale
To 40 in. (1 m)
Leaves grow in whorls of 4 around the stem.

Death Camas
Zigadenus elegans
To 28 in. (70 cm)
Star-shaped, green-centered flowers bloom in a long terminal cluster. Plant is highly poisonous.

Wild Strawberry
Fragaria virginiana
Stems to 8 in. (20 cm)
Creeping plant has 5-petalled flowers that are succeeded by the familiar fruit.

Cow Parsnip
Heracleum spp.
To 9 ft. (2.7 m)
Grows in moist soils. Creamy white flowers bloom in dense, flattened clusters.

Canada Mayflower
Maianthemum canadense
To 6 in. (15 cm)
Star-shaped flowers bloom in a spire-like cluster.

Nodding Trillium
Trillium cernuum
To 20 in. (50 cm)

Meadow Anemone
Anemone canadensis
To 2 ft. (60 cm)

Sego Lily
Calochortus nuttallii
To 18 in. (45 cm)

Philadelphia Fleabane
Erigeron philadelphicus
To 3 ft. (90 cm)

Yucca
Yucca glauca
To 4 ft. (1.2 m)

Starflower
Smilacina stellata
To 2 ft. (60 cm)
Tiny white flowers are star-shaped.

Wintergreen
Pyrola spp.
To 8 in. (20 cm)
Nodding, waxy, white flowers bloom along stalk.

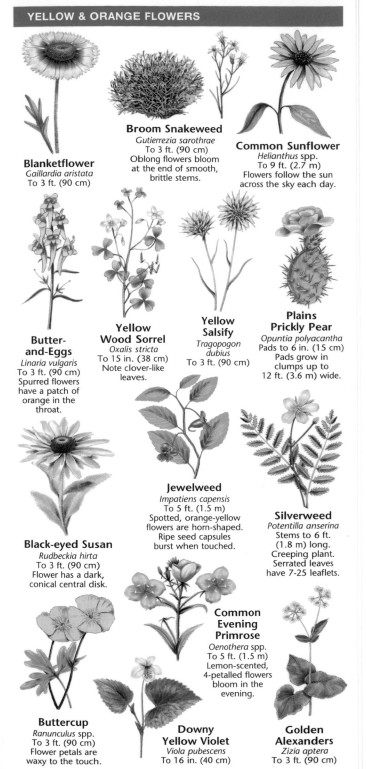

Phlox
Phlox spp.
To 20 in. (50 cm)
Five-petalled, yellow-centered flowers may be white, yellow, pink, red or lavender. Grows in sprawling clusters.

Field Bindweed
Convolvulus spp.
To 3 ft. (90 cm)
Told by arrowhead-shaped leaves and white to pink, funnel-shaped flowers.

Jack-in-the-Pulpit
Arisaema triphyllum
To 3 ft. (90 cm)
Club-like stem is surrounded by a curving, green to purplish hood.

False Dandelion
Agoseris glauca
To 28 in. (70 cm)

Marsh Marigold
Caltha palustris
To 2 ft. (60 cm)
Aquatic plant has large, heart-shaped leaves.

Yellow Lady's Slipper
Cypripedium calceolus
To 28 in. (70 cm)

Leafy Spurge
Euphorbia esula
To 3 ft. (90 cm)
Small green flowers are surrounded by yellow-green, petal-like bracts.

Wood Lily
Lilium philadelphicum
To 28 in. (70 cm)

Yellow Coneflower
Ratibida columnifera
To 4 ft. (1.2 m)

Slender Locoweed
Oxytropis campestris
To 10 in. (25 cm)
Yellow, pea-shaped flowers bloom in May-June.

Yellow Wild Buckwheat
Eriogonum flavum
To 16 in. (40 cm)

Wild Licorice
Glycyrrhiza lepidota
To 40 in. (1 m)

Western Wallflower
Erysimum asperum
To 2 ft. (60 cm)
Found in open forests and meadows.

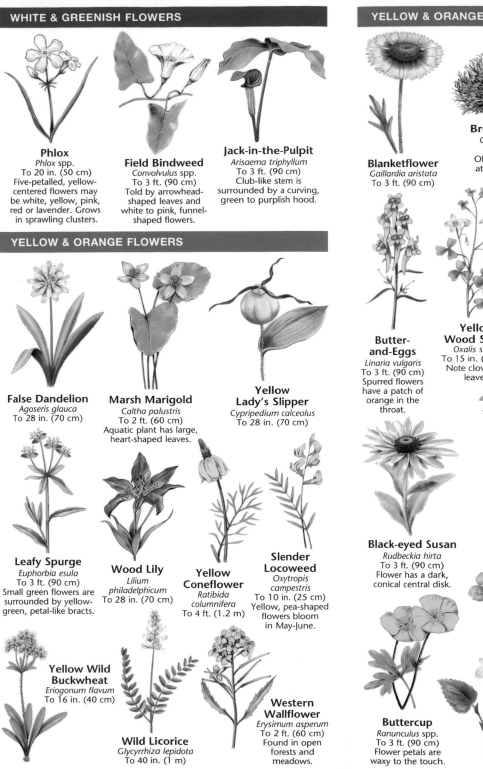

Blanketflower
Gaillardia aristata
To 3 ft. (90 cm)

Broom Snakeweed
Gutierrezia sarothrae
To 3 ft. (90 cm)
Oblong flowers bloom at the end of smooth, brittle stems.

Common Sunflower
Helianthus spp.
To 9 ft. (2.7 m)
Flowers follow the sun across the sky each day.

Butter-and-Eggs
Linaria vulgaris
To 3 ft. (90 cm)
Spurred flowers have a patch of orange in the throat.

Yellow Wood Sorrel
Oxalis stricta
To 15 in. (38 cm)
Note clover-like leaves.

Yellow Salsify
Tragopogon dubius
To 3 ft. (90 cm)

Plains Prickly Pear
Opuntia polyacantha
Pads to 6 in. (15 cm)
Pads grow in clumps up to 12 ft. (3.6 m) wide.

Black-eyed Susan
Rudbeckia hirta
To 3 ft. (90 cm)
Flower has a dark, conical central disk.

Jewelweed
Impatiens capensis
To 5 ft. (1.5 m)
Spotted, orange-yellow flowers are horn-shaped. Ripe seed capsules burst when touched.

Silverweed
Potentilla anserina
Stems to 6 ft. (1.8 m) long
Creeping plant. Serrated leaves have 7-25 leaflets.

Common Evening Primrose
Oenothera spp.
To 5 ft. (1.5 m)
Lemon-scented, 4-petalled flowers bloom in the evening.

Buttercup
Ranunculus spp.
To 3 ft. (90 cm)
Flower petals are waxy to the touch.

Downy Yellow Violet
Viola pubescens
To 16 in. (40 cm)

Golden Alexanders
Zizia aptera
To 3 ft. (90 cm)

Spreading Dogbane
Apocynum androsaemifolium
To 20 in. (50 cm)

Columbine
Aquilegia canadensis
To 2 ft. (60 cm)

Milkweed
Asclepias spp.
To 4 ft. (1.2 m)
Leaves and stem are sticky.

Nodding Thistle
Carduus nutans
To 9 ft. (2.7 m)

Rocky Mountain Bee Plant
Cleome serrulata
To 5 ft. (1.5 m)
Leaves have 3 narrow leaflets.

Scarlet Gaura
Guara coccinea
To 2 ft. (60 cm)

Old Man's Whiskers
Geum triflorum
To 16 in. (40 cm)

Pincushion Cactus
Coryphantha vivipara
To 6 ft. (1.8 m)

Purple Coneflower
Echinacea angustifolia
To 30 in. (75 cm)

Wild Bergamot
Monarda fistulosa
To 4 ft. (1.2 m)

Purple Prairie Clover
Dalea purpurea
To 3 ft. (90 cm)

Hairy Four-o-clock
Mirabilis hirsuta
To 3 ft. (90 cm)

Water Smartweed
Polygonum amphibium
Stems to 4 ft. (1.2 m) long
Aquatic plant blooms in nearshore waters.

Fireweed
Chamerion angustifolium
To 10 ft. (3 m)
Common in open woodlands and waste areas.

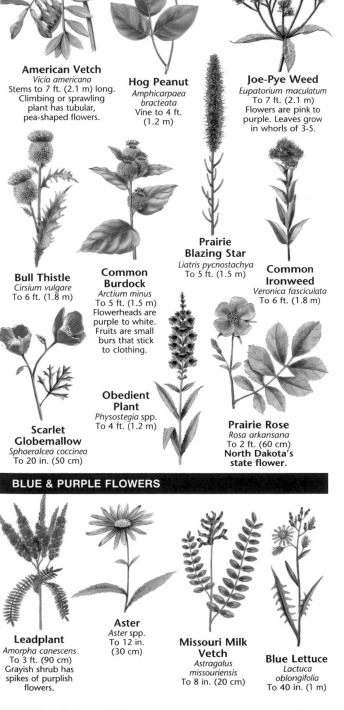

American Vetch
Vicia americana
Stems to 7 ft. (2.1 m) long.
Climbing or sprawling plant has tubular, pea-shaped flowers.

Hog Peanut
Amphicarpaea bracteata
Vine to 4 ft. (1.2 m)

Joe-Pye Weed
Eupatorium maculatum
To 7 ft. (2.1 m)
Flowers are pink to purple. Leaves grow in whorls of 3-5.

Bull Thistle
Cirsium vulgare
To 6 ft. (1.8 m)

Common Burdock
Arctium minus
To 5 ft. (1.5 m)
Flowerheads are purple to white. Fruits are small burs that stick to clothing.

Prairie Blazing Star
Liatris pycnostachya
To 5 ft. (1.5 m)

Common Ironweed
Veronica fasciculata
To 6 ft. (1.8 m)

Scarlet Globemallow
Sphaeralcea coccinea
To 20 in. (50 cm)

Obedient Plant
Physostegia spp.
To 4 ft. (1.2 m)

Prairie Rose
Rosa arkansana
To 2 ft. (60 cm)
North Dakota's state flower.

Leadplant
Amorpha canescens
To 3 ft. (90 cm)
Grayish shrub has spikes of purplish flowers.

Aster
Aster spp.
To 12 in. (30 cm)

Missouri Milk Vetch
Astragalus missouriensis
To 8 in. (20 cm)

Blue Lettuce
Lactuca oblongifolia
To 40 in. (1 m)

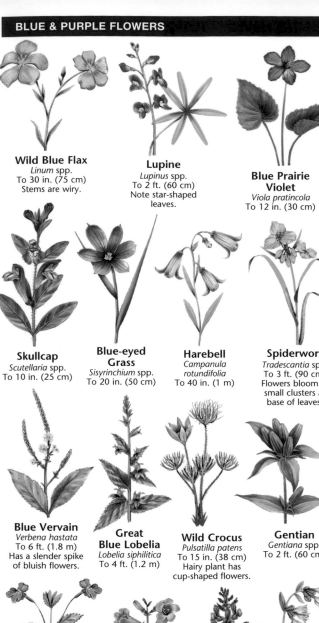
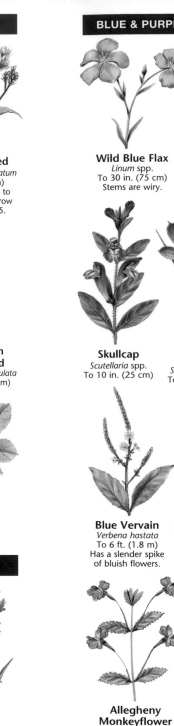
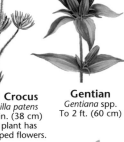

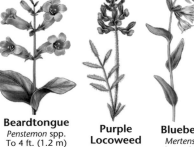

Wild Blue Flax
Linum spp.
To 30 in. (75 cm)
Stems are wiry.

Lupine
Lupinus spp.
To 2 ft. (60 cm)
Note star-shaped leaves.

Blue Prairie Violet
Viola pratincola
To 12 in. (30 cm)

Skullcap
Scutellaria spp.
To 10 in. (25 cm)

Blue-eyed Grass
Sisyrinchium spp.
To 20 in. (50 cm)

Harebell
Campanula rotundifolia
To 40 in. (1 m)

Spiderwort
Tradescantia spp.
To 3 ft. (90 cm)
Flowers bloom in small clusters at base of leaves.

Blue Vervain
Verbena hastata
To 6 ft. (1.8 m)
Has a slender spike of bluish flowers.

Great Blue Lobelia
Lobelia siphilitica
To 4 ft. (1.2 m)

Wild Crocus
Pulsatilla patens
To 15 in. (38 cm)
Hairy plant has cup-shaped flowers.

Gentian
Gentiana spp.
To 2 ft. (60 cm)

Allegheny Monkeyflower
Mimulus ringens
To 3 ft. (90 cm)
Bluish, yellow-centered flowers have a puffy lower lip.

Beardtongue
Penstemon spp.
To 4 ft. (1.2 m)
Lower lip and throat of flower is 'bearded' with fine hairs.

Purple Locoweed
Oxytropis lambertii
To 16 in. (40 cm)

Bluebells
Mertensia lanceolata
To 12 in. (30 cm)